ENTREPRENEURSHIP

FROM AN ENGINEER'S PERSPECTIVE

RAMESH K MAHADEV

CEO & Founder, Trividtrans Private Limited

Mechatronics Engineer & Motorsport Enthusiast

Passionate Entrepreneur @ Entrepreneur Lifestyle Hub

www.rameshkmahadev.com

DEDICATED TO

All The Passionate Entrepreneurs Who
Want To Contribute Something Best To
The Humanity And On A Mission To
Impact The World In A Great Positive Way

CONTENTS

Taking Decision At The Right Time Is More Important Than Taking The Right Decision.

TIME SPACE ENERGY

Chapter One

Taking decision at the right time is more important than taking the right decision, Most of the thing we acknowledge with our senses may make sense more than what we simply think. Each time you want to make a decision, each time you want to take a step forward, each time you want to re-invent yourself, you may step out of that decision making position with excuses because of your procrastination attitude or even some people may project themselves as lazy to the world but the main reason will be the fear, some people have the fear of failure and some people have the fear of success. Yes, some peoples do exist where instead of thinking the reality "If you are the only wisest man in the room, you should probably get out from there" they will think "If I'll become the only wisest man in the room, probably they may throw me out of the room", and this fear of being lonely at the top may stop some peoples from making decision.

When I was in school I used to wonder a lot about this world, our existence in this world, if you remember your primary school days, if you are fan of science your one of the questions would be "If earth is like a ball, if we stand on earth with our foot on ground, What about the peoples on the other side of the earth and how they will be....?", luckily I got a great physics teacher who explained me how gravity works, the planets , the space and all the basics. So which is my first crush with physics. And in my mind the question which is live from that days to today be "Is time travel possible....?" Well, I will definitely not gonna discus weather it is possible or not (I think it is possible, yet to figure out how...? Oops I should not discus..!), But to make you understand the need for making your decision as soon as possible using a scientific proof.

Let me explain this with figure, A three dimensional system where consider X as Time, Y as Space and Z as Energy, origin will be your present time i.e. Reality. Each and every second of your life YZ plane that is your space Energy plane, which will be moving in x direction with time. And in each instance of life you need to make a decision knowingly or unknowingly, i.e. out of multiple squares in the YZ plane i.e. you're Life, you select any one square to live for that moment and that is what decision means scientifically. So if you observe carefully, the moment you chose to live a moment it becomes your realty. Then that reality becomes the new origin from where a new timeline will start. And the cycle repeats and the life continues....well, felt like something just flew over your head. Let me try to put it in other way to understand easily

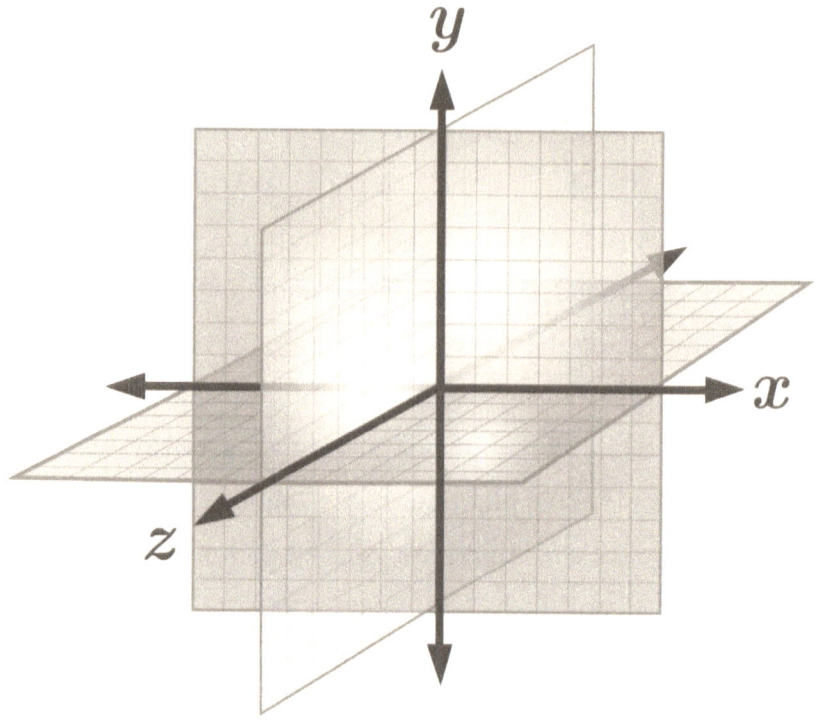

Figure 1: X - Time, Y - Space and Z - Energy.

What I was trying to tell is similar to Choosing the way at each road intersections when you are driving. Where, from the end of a single road multiple roads start, you can chose a best one or a bad one, but all the proceeding ways will be associated with the choices you made throughout the journey.

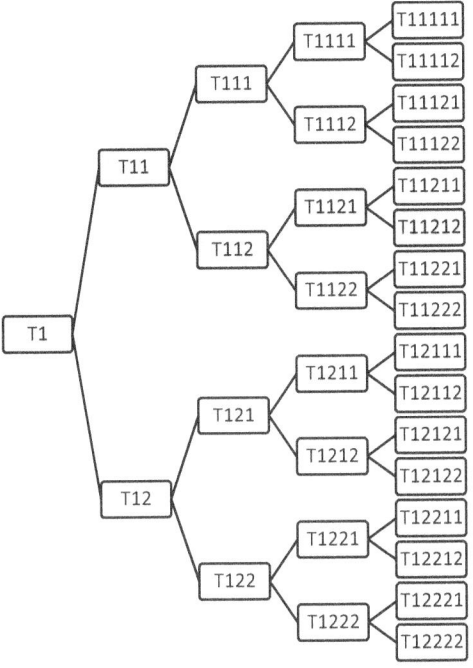

Figure 2: T represents time and all the numbers represent the events accord

As you can see in the figure 2, the first choice you made was T1 followed by T11, T112, T1121, and T11212...and so on, but remember "The options you can live are bounded by only a limit called infinity". Even though if you are not making any decision, "Not making a decision become your default decision costing you an unused valuable moment of your life which will never return".

In the example above I used an alphanumeric code to present all the options available at each and every moment, this are all like a traceable codes, where if you want to deal with a critical situation, you can always trace back to source code of you past where you faced a similar challenge and take that lessons to tackle new "Only if you successfully made a decision at that time". It's not about the decisions are correct or incorrect, because taken decision leave you with two probability which you can predict and act accordingly. But probability doesn't exists with the decisions which were never take.

By the way, you may think how anyone can live on this planet without making decisions, you are thinking normal. If you are making a right thing which feed your passion and let you live your entire life with a smile on face, If you are making a daring decision to get fit in self defined period, If you are making a caring decision to be a better Son / Daughter, Husband/wife, Father/ Mother, Brother /sister, a friend to see the smile on the faces which care for you, If you are decided to hustle in your free time to go extra mile in your life, If you are making a decision to move away from a group of spoiled minds to protect your positive vibes, If you decided to dive on a new startup venture which can contribute something good for humanity. Then each and every moment you are selecting the right coordinates to live on and I'm sure that the plot created by those source codes that you created through your decisions, will definitely take you to the peak of Success from where, the view will be worth your each precious moments exponentially that you decided to work with instead of letting them go....!

Until You Jump, Don't Expect To Learn How It Feels To Fly...!

PRE IGNITION

Chapter Two

Until you jump, don't expect to learn how it feels to fly...! You don't have all the time in this advanced world, only few are lucky enough to see their grandchildren. Then why are you waiting for something to happen, some peoples tell have patience and wait for the good thing to happen, by doing so you will become only Wantrepreneur. Good thing never happen by waiting, good thing happen only when you work for them. Execution is everything in this world so stop waiting in the hell until the next door opens, ring the bell if not kick the door in front of you with all the potential powered by your passion. Be an opportunist; never let a door shut until you feel it is not your dish. In addition, let me tell you, you can have only two options in front of you all the time. - 1. Here is an opportunity waiting for me. 2. Here is an opportunity to create opportunities, as I cannot find one.

If you are an automotive person or what we called motor head, you will have idea about how an engine works. Let me explain in short for the once for whom this is not their favorite candy. Basically Engine of your vehicle convert the fuel energy to mechanical energy by burning the fuel in the engine cylinder. There is a part which provide spark to ignite the fuel air mixture in the engine which is called sparkplug.

As I worked in motorsport teams during my under graduation collage time where our team had built amazing race grade vehicles, and I got an opportunity to work on Engine and transmission system where I tuned my knowledge on Automobiles. As we were working with the stock engines available in the market, we needed a serious power upgradation as those engines were made for limited power output.

One interesting fact about automobile engines is there always exits an untapped percentage of power reserved with the engine which is never touched. To convert your normal engine to a beast, to tap that reserved power we go for something called Engine Tuning.

One of the major thing what we do is change the timing of spark (We do some other changes too, but this is the major one...). Normally The spark should be given when the piston reaches the top dead center (top end) of the Engine cylinder, What we do is we advance the spark timing by fraction of second i.e. the spark is given even before the piston reaches the top dead center which in turns results in decreased combustion timing contributing to better efficiency and a great power to vehicle. By this tuning we convert a normal performing vehicle to a race ready beast. You can find the difference between the normal ignition and the advanced ignition in the following figure.

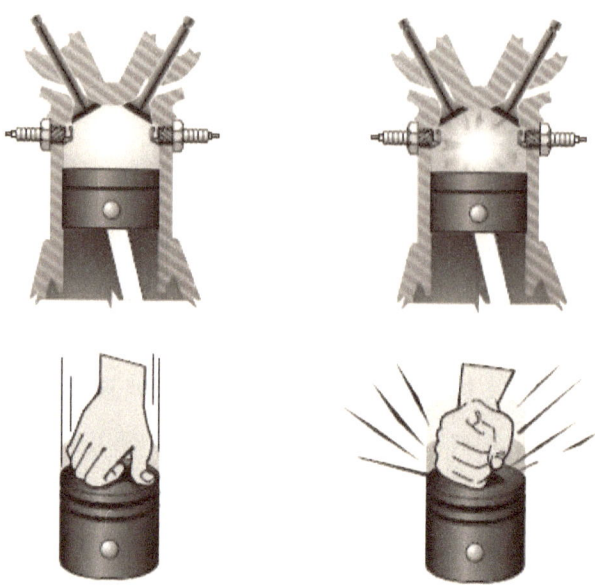

Figure 3: Normal ignition (Left) Advanced Ignition (Right)

You may be thinking why this Grease monkey is talking about all this engine stuff. No, I don't want you to go and advance the timing of your engine ignition now…. (It is really amazing if you do that to your car…it converts the beauties into serious performing beasts…).

What I want you to do is run before you are ready, as the word entrepreneur define itself, as the "The one who jumps before ready, and learn on the way down, how to fly", and I also want you to remember…. Learning how to fly after jumping is as important as jumping, make sure you do that before you hit the ground.

It's not that simple as it sounds, Rushing the process, playing the game before entering the podium, ready to take that shock waves of failures and abstractions. What you have to learn about life is, it's not about the place you reach, and it's about the path you traveled... the more you rush, the more time you get and the more distance you cover. Instead of waiting to make something perfect, make something and perfect it over a period of time.

If you observe any vehicle advertisements, documentary, magazine...They will definitely mention like "Tested over million miles...", "Tested over 7 continental conditions...", "Pushing the limits of testing to extreme..." Did you ever wonder why they are telling so; the universal truth is you can make something perfect only when you figure out the extreme limit, which can handle. The continues process of trailing, testing, tracking the feedback back to source to correct the cause and continue, this is what which make things what they are...whether it's a car or you.

You Can Never Be A Better Leader With A Mindset Of A Noble Element.

THEORY OF REACTIVITY

Chapter Three

You can never be a better leader with a mindset of a noble element .when you can run around your dream office, talking and spreading smiles among your employees, cheering up for development like a teen dancing on his toes with full passion. Why you want to corner yourself with a tag of strict boss. If you really look out who are the experts in making friends and liked by everyone, the answer is kids. They never hesitate to approach, never think before sharing a story, never expect anything from anyone...but they receive all the love and positivity. When you start being curious like a kid, you start enjoying others stories. Peoples no more get connect to the person who tell calculations, they connect to the stories you tell. As we know the chemical reactivity of a material increases, it starts building bonds with other chemicals, resulting in creating new compounds. As you start creating bonds with the peoples around you, the new compounds what we called ideas, solutions, innovations start to flow.

Being this said you should also have control over the reaction because some reaction produces useful compounds, some will not. If we consider the simplest example of Hydrogen and oxygen. As we all know Hydrogen can be used as a fuel and oxygen is necessary for combustion of anything, when they both combined in the form of water, it can shut the fire.

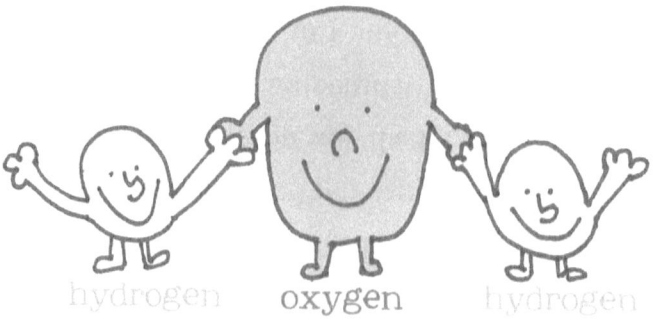
hydrogen   oxygen   hydrogen

Always there exists a positive side and negative side for a person, the side that you try to explore more will start to contribute more. With the same set of peoples in your team you can start criticizing on negativities of all resulting in the creation of harmful compound or you may choose to explore the creativity, talent and hardworking positivity of your team mates by appreciating their attitude and create an amazing product.

Whenever you get an opportunity to work with a team, always be on toe because the ideas may get emerge in their purest form from individual but the proper nourishment can only be possible by a great set of peoples around you. In this decade most of the young entrepreneurs started emerging with ideas, the fact is ideas are useless unless they are executed, so most of young minds will stop with the idea because they have the fear to execute, they have the fear of failing, they have fear to approach peoples and ask for help, they have the fear of starting from the bottom.

Think about someone who is reactive as we discussed a couple of minutes before, who is like kid, who never hesitate, who is an expert in bond creation, who can convey his stories flawlessly with ease. Even though if he can come up with a small idea he got all the potential to be a successful entrepreneur. The only reason is because for a non-reactive wantrepreneur it may take more time or May not possible to make a conversion "My idea to our plan" but the reactive entrepreneur can get to this point effortlessly. It doesn't mean that you are not putting efforts in getting this done, but you are enjoying to being adopted to this new lifestyle with your full potential....when you are enjoying something, you won't feel like you are putting efforts.

Future Fiction Is No More A Fantasy When You Are The One Creating It.

TWO DIMENSIONAL FICTION

Chapter Four

Future fiction is no more a fantasy when you are the one creating it. By the way, I am a great fan of marvel studios and my all-time favorite character is Tony stark the iron man, the reason is all the power he got are results of his own creation... (Because of Robert Downey Jr.'s amazing screenplay too...). Even though the iron man is a fictional character in the movie or comics, the flying suite is no more just a fictional costume, As the company Gravity industries from UK founded by an inventor Richard browning successfully developed jet power-driven iron man suit which can actually perform like iron man suite in the movie... (But it's not weaponized yet).by the way I take this chance to thank Mr. Stan lee for making our childhood awesome with his creative characters, Love you man....

What I was trying to tell is no fiction in this world is untouchable, only distance, which is stopping it to come to reality, is only people's mindset. Until your dream looks like a fiction to normal people, you are not dreaming big enough. You are just experiencing an urge to win the rat race. The person who tells his dream in front of peoples are most likely to achieve it, because every time your spirit drops or a night party excites you, you feel like some invisible voice is laughing at you, which gives a kick to jumpstart your hustling.

How many of you believe in the fantasy ideas of Mr. Elon Musk....?. I strongly do believe his ideas of colonizing & building the metropolitan cities on mars, crazy idea of using a nuke to heat up the planet. Want to travel in Hyperloop under the cities, space tourism, neural link, sending tesla car to space, building a crazy flamethrower with a please don't buy sticker on it......and what else. Because he know all the ideas, which he said will definitely be executed because he is the one who is doing it. If some can do things which looks impossible, what's the boundary for you? You got all the potential...? You got all tools you want...? Are you dare enough to dream big...? YES, definitely, you can and you will.

The next thing is converting your dreams to plans by tailoring your wishes with the realistic time line. Making money is a dream, making forty million in next two years with a monthly income of three million from my two active and four passive income sources is a plan.

If you ever pitched before an investor or a bank for rising fund or for an association you know, the major two thing they look for is your company compliance and next five or three-year plan. The compliances shows your discipline and the growth, the plan shows your expectations and the steps to be taken for the execution to meet the expectation. So well planned pitch can place you ahead of the competition, well-planned dreams will make your fictions reality.

Always remember this "Failing to plan is same as

that of planning to fail" and from next time keep correcting everyone you care by asking them to replace dream by plan, when they say "I have a dream of becoming something...".

Never Lose Your
Acceleration In An
Excitement Of
Changing The Gear.

TRANSIT LIKE MULTICLUTCH

Chapter Five

Never lose your acceleration in an excitement of changing the gear. Hopefully you start understanding my automotive influenced philosophies... (Even the automotive world is as crazy as hell....trust me). Whenever we drive a vehicle with manual gear shifter, we always need to speed down while shifting from one gear to other gear. That's because each time you shift the gear, the old gear will get disengaged and the new gear will get engaged, so to cut the power flow during that processes of gear changing, we use something called clutch. So each time you press the clutch the power flow is cut down resulting in speed down of vehicle. This is a big drawback, which need to be addressed to get a better performance. And this achieved by some of the popular technologies like CVT (Continuously variable transmission) and Duel clutch mechanism. Just to simplify for the non-technical guys this technology simply achieve one thing, instead of sudden gear disengage, it start to disengage one gear slowly, at the same time the other gear start to engage slowly, by the moment one gear is completely disengaged other gear is completely engaged. This ensure the continuous flow of power and your vehicle will never accelerate down while changing the gear. Nowadays Almost all the performance vehicles are feature with this advanced technology

Do accept my apology if you think I'm exhibiting a bit extra love for automobiles... (I couldn't control....lol). What I want you to do is learn to transit as smooth as duel clutch. As per human psychology, No one can accept a drastic change even though we all know change is the only constant in this world. When you are on a job or venture or a challenge. Try to get on multiple things, but remember not at once. Try out all the things you think you should even if you think you may get lots of path holes and road humps on your way because that's the only way to check whether it's your plate are not, figure out what suits you....

Something you should start is a side hustle which will pay you some extra bucks for something which you enjoy doing it in your spare time. Create content, start using your social media to go for that extra miles you always wanted to, start writing a blog if you are a good writer, try to express our thoughts or your creativity through your words, write a book, and create podcasts. As I said, you should transit from that old life with limited colors to these things which can help you live this amazing Entrepreneur lifestyle.

Start to invest your saving or earning may be through trading stocks (I'll discus a bit in the next chapter too), purchasing and flipping business, real estate, online store, e-commerce delivery service etc. The only startup kit every entrepreneur need to start something in this world moving toward near future cyborg tech is a laptop / smartphone, Wi-Fi / Internet connection , a Brain , an idea and a strong will to make it happen.

And some other place you can invest, the no.1 is you should invest is on books and learning. Because the books you read makes you. Always remember this two rules, "Learn to Earn" and "Read to Lead". book is one of the best technology human ever witnessed. As we were in our school, learn from your mistakes, but what you need to understand is life is too short to waste it by trailing all by your own, learn from the experience who walked the same or similar path. And always remember the final choice is yours. If all who tried doing what you want you do failed doesn't mean you can't, because you are different from all of them.

You may heard some quotes or red some line somewhere like "At the end of the day, both a hundred dollar watch and a million dollar watch shows the same timing, both Toyota and rolls Royce can carry the same peoples, both the rich and the poor will die one day....the true happiness is in being healthy, being helpful, being simple" please don't get fooled by this quotes, everything you see in the form of quotes are not true. This are the finest examples of excuse given by one who don't dare to achieve something big. I agree with a fact that money can't buy happiness but money can buy things, the things which will make you happy, the things which will get smiles on others face, the thing that helps to keep you healthy, the things which helps for your personal growth. And always question why to choose between materialistic freedom and emotional freedom when you have the desire and capability to master both.

Think in this way, if you can help a thousand by being a millionaire, how many you can help if you become billionaire.....?. Contributing to humanity is what matters at the end. So be weaponized yourself as early as possible with wisdom, health, wealth and happiness.

Always Follow Your
Mind With Permission
From Heart.

BRAIN HEART WAIT

Chapter Six

Always follow your mind with permission from heart.
Let's get back on track for a while (By any means track means race track for me by default...). So every gasoline powered car will have an engine, and there is something called ECU i.e. Engine/Electronic control Unit. Every function of the Engine is monitored and controlled by ECU. If there is any problem with ECU, the engine will end up in trouble. When there is any problem in engine, ECU

helps to trouble shoot and correct that problem.

So there is no much difference between your brain and ECU, Heart and engine. When you are driving, you will feel the roar of the car, the vibration, the momentum and everything is generated by the engine and all are examined and refined by ECU. If you closely recognize all the feelings are generated by your heart, but you should make sure your brain is refining and correcting what you feel.

"Your thoughts are controlled by your feelings, your feelings are controlled by you thinking, and so which makes both interdependent," said by Sadhguru. That's damn true.so remember, Always Go with your heart if mind permits and you should not proceed only with mind when heart say no. Do believe in your gut.

Let me tell you where exactly you need to keep your

sentiments bit far, it's in stock market. Where the feeling of losing money makes you to lose more, and the feel of secure from winning makes you win small.

For example say a person buys a stock for 100 Rupees, and the stock value start to decrease, let say it drops to 98 Rupees.so the person start feeling sad and wish it should increase in next call, but unfortunately again it falls to 96 Rupees but he think let us hope for the next call, it may wait at least it go backs to 100 rupees with no loss but again it falls to 94 rupees. That person decides no point in waiting so he sell it for 94 Rupees with 6 Rupees loss. In the other scenario when he buy the stock for 100 Rupees, say it raises for 102 rupees he is happy because the plots are in his direction, next if it falls back to 101 Rupees he may feel insecure and sell by making 1 rupees profit. Think if both the trade was done by a same person with emotional attachment with the variations in the market, when he win, he makes only 1 rupees, when he lose he is likely to lose 6 rupees.

So always remember when to listen to your emotions, when to not.

Nothing Happens Until Something Moves.

LOOKS LIE TOO

Chapter Seven

Nothing happens until something moves, by the way Einstein said that and it's very true. And nowadays all the moves you see or all the things what you see are not what they are. Let me explain you with a basic physics to make it more interesting, consider two peoples who is standing on a vehicle and they are throwing a ball upwards.

We can see both the scenarios in the pictures in the next page but first tell me what you think about these two players below.

Let's name them Mr. Left and Mr. Right. So what do you think, both looks almost similar, so both may be good at throwing the ball, both can perform similar, Right. This is the most likely answer you may be thinking off. Let us agree both poses the same amount of potential and both apply the same amount of effort to throw the ball upwards, and for both hard work pays off, luckily both the balls thrown by two reached the same height. So let us look at one more set of pictures of both the player

So, what do you think whose work payed more?

Mr. Left successfully achieved a height successfully, but Mr. Right covered a large slop while applying the same effort as that of Mr. Left, which makes the overall outcome of Mr. Rights effort pay drastically more compared to Mr. Left outcome.

By the way this is explained as a Relative projectile motions in terms of physics. In this example Mr. Left resembles the person who trade time for money, an employee, a person who depends on a single source of income who always works for money. Mr. Right clearly indicate the Right mindset of an entrepreneur, an investor, a great business man who always trade value for money who always make money work for him. The normal peoples like Mr. Left always celebrate the one dimensional success and thinks the height is their only priority. But the Successful peoples like Mr. Right always create a platform which helps them to achieve the two dimensional freedom, where first they trade value for money, then they make money works for them to make more money.

And one more thing is don't get fooled by the posts you see in social media that's why I shown you the first picture of Mr. Left and Mr. Right. Nobody is posting their failure and the successful never post his next move until they make it, only open minds can see the bigger pictures. By the way don't forget to create a platform that will help you to cover you some distance while you are busy in reaching a height in one dimension, start your side hustles and keep them active.

Don't Confuse
Productivity With
Being Busy.

BEING COOL IS NOT ALWAYS COOL

Chapter Eight

Don't confuse productivity with being busy, you can realize when we look at the way people feel for not getting what they want after putting lot of effort, let's take a moment to understand this. If you consider any material, when it comes to its electric conductive property we can majorly divide them into three categories. Conductors, Nonconductors and semiconductors, among them let us eliminate Nonconductors first as they represents the people who want to play safe, get settled for what they have, who live by the principle " let's keep our dreams just to dream", comfort is everything. My concern is for Conductors and semiconductors, if you look at the properties of conductors they are the excellent conductors of electricity at room temperature but as the temperature increases the conductivity of the material starts to decrease. On the other hand, let us consider semiconductors, this exhibit a different property where at normal temperature there conductivity is comparatively low but as the temperature increase their conductivity also increases.

So why I'm I explaining the basics of electronics to you, not because I'm a mechatronics engineer but to explain the reality of this competitive world. All the employees, working class, people who trade their time for money comes under conductor category. Because when you live in employee category while you are in a job, you are earning a decent money to live your life to enjoy weekends, you are feeling independent because you got a life after 9 to 5 work, you may feel or people may feel you are doing great, this is what room temperature means. Once you find out your salary is a bribe to forget your dreams, the statement "you are well settled" means you are a ship ready to sink, the moment your bills kills the excitement of your salary slip, once you realize no one is irreplaceable in this competitive world...the very next moment you start to feel the increase in temperature and you start feeling like you are no more the same person who used to dream of owning a Bentley, who dreamed of becoming an astronaut in the childhood.

You start feeling the guilty feel as a murderer who killed that child dream, but in some people's life, by the time they realize, their life journey will almost reached its end. Why I'm concerned about this category is they are willing to work, put their effort but somewhere diverted on their way to different direction. It doesn't mean that everyone should become entrepreneurs, it means if you are not leaving your life to its full, then you need to rethink before you revisit your office.

Let us consider semiconductor now, if an active person is given with a simple work it's kind of boring to him. Some peoples mindset is preprogrammed like that, but we don't know how to recode it...Most of the students are associated with a problem or what I call talent

(Because I belonged to same category in my collage days...), where the only productive time to complete a task is a minute before deadline. I'm not telling you to postpone your work to deadline but to make you to understand the priorities. If you observe, most of the great entrepreneurs keep themselves as productive as possible by keeping themselves engaged in exploring several opportunities.

As you start working for yourself, as you start working on an idea that triggered in your mind, that dream for which you are creating a plan to accomplish. You always find a way to keep you engaged which means you no more feel that you are not a good conductor because you are out of that comfort room temperature Zone and each atom of your thought is powered by that increased temperature of your positive vibes to achieve what's in your mind.

The only reason people confuse there productivity with being busy is because they successfully fail to understand their what, why, how, who, when of their goals. It does not matter how faster you are running if you are not sure about the direction, you may end up where you least expected.

You can relate this to a startup, unless you know what is your idea, why it is better than existing solution, how can we make it more better, who are our potential customers, what's the timeline we are talking about. Without knowing any one of this, even you did an amazing job on developing a great business plan after weeks of hard work, the chances of your startup success still stands near nil. Which doesn't mean that you didn't put your best, but you missed something on the way to make others best. So don't be that literal unfortunate guy. Be like semiconductor, be more productive, no room for room temperature drama, only conductivity of motivated work culture.

The Impact Is More
When The Time Of
Force Applied Is Less.

LET'S TALK NUCLEAR

Chapter Nine

The impact is more when the time of force applied is less Never extend the process even though the time permits you. So most of you heard about nukes, one of the tool which is actually preventing the third world war by inducing mutual fear at least for time being. The nuclear concept is all about trapping the energy of an atom when its brakes or combines with other atom, by the way for non-science fans, If two atoms nucleuses combines together it's called fusion and if one atom nucleus splits into two it's called Nuclear fission by the way this nuclear reactions are the reasons which keeps our sun bright and all the stars too. Moreover, all the normal chemical reactions are involved only with the outer or the orbiter elements but nuclear reaction is what happens with core of the atom.

Always remember, the group of people around you can affect your performance, that is true to an extent but it's not the complete truth. They can tell what you should do, they may try to induce some habits which can eventually become your routine, they may change your opinions on some decisions you made, but they can only access your outer orbit. But you are the one who can make it or break it, because at the end, all the orbits exists only if the nucleus wants them to exist. Stop playing with outer electrons and get into your core that is where actual you can create something, find something, which no one never found, Respect the opinions but evaluate once before accepting.

Complete the things ASAP, because the starting early is important but if you take long to accomplish what you want, the latecomer can be the first finisher. In this 5G world you no need to stop to get lost, just slow down a bit, you will be already in lagging phase. So get things done quicker, as the time taken to complete something decreases, you will try to concentrate each second you work on it, which eventually contributes to excellent productivity which will surprise you. I'm not a fan of waterways but always I like its two principles. One, an ocean of water can't sink a ship even though ship is completely surrounded by it unless it enters inside the ship. Two, Longer the sail time, higher the probability of change in path due to side winds if not taken care off.

No Interference Is
Better Than
Destructive
Interference.

WAVE THEORY

Chapter Ten

No interference is better than destructive interference. Let's talk about music, world-class noise cancelling technology is engineered to block out distractions, so you can enjoy your music with nothing in the way. Many music Acoustic device manufacturers who make headphone, earphones, home theaters, automotive interior sound systems are working on this Noise Cancelling technology. So its basic principle is very simple and that is called wave interference, by the way there are two types of interference constructive interference and destructive interference.

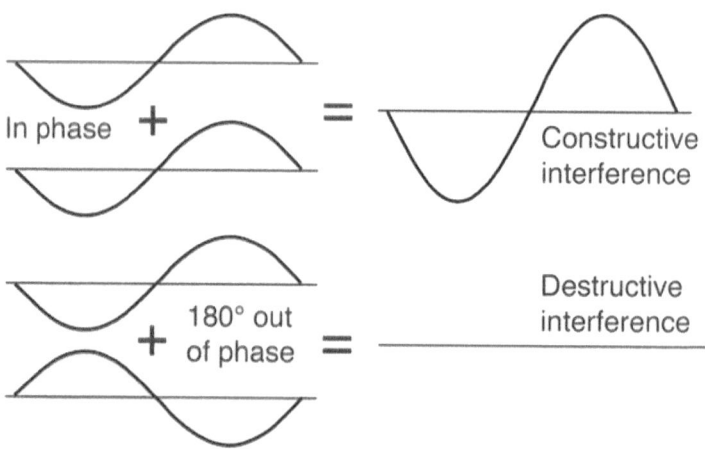

It's very simple, as we all know sound is a form of wave, this happens with all the waves starting from water waves to electromagnetic waves. Whenever the two waves which are in same phase interfere, the amplitude (height) of resultant wave will be higher than both individuals i.e. sum of the amplitudes of those two which are combined. Whenever both the waves are out of phase the resultant wave will have a less amplitude or No amplitude at all.

I really don't want to explain my engineering subject DSP (Digital Signal Processing) here, but we can understand something easily from here ... (Even though it's hard for me to understand actual DSP).

There is a phrase "Surround yourself with people who are in same mission as you" and I thank god because I found few around me. Its absolute true. If you are discussing with the person with a negative mindset for everything always remember you will end up in destructive interference because they have problem for every solution, if you are the wisest man in the room you are in the wrong room, get out of there ASAP.

When you have aspiration of achieving something great, when you are ready to welcome lots of wealth in your life, if you are ready to tap your reserved potential to go that extra mile, that constructive interference with the people with the positive mindset as you can become an alarm which alerts you each time you slow down, can act as a machine of idea creation when you want to do something new. This is possible only if you are smart enough to choose the right wave to interfere with.

Be a damn Wi-Fi broadband, don't be just a user, it's funny but reality. Most of the peoples spend almost their entire life with a limited subscription pack. Get the hell out of there. Don't die before you are dead. Be a broadband and have a control on your subscribers so you can always welcome positive waves by filtering the negative or noise. The most important thing is, always make sure you enjoy your Music of Passion on the way to success.

CONCLUSION

When you look at the sky at night for 5 minutes, you start seeing more stars than on 1st second, if you keep looking for 15 minutes you start observing patterns and shapes created by connecting the stars, some creates objects out of stars and some creates animals out of clouds, All in their minds. As humans we have the greatest power of creating what we want, what we love, what we want to be. Sky is no more the limit as we witnessed footprints on moon. All you want to do is start working towards your passion to create a great wealth for yourself and the peoples around you, start investing on yourself through learning, grow your network, learn to give without expectations, learn to use your will and skill to convert those passionate dreams into reality and start living your life in Passionate Entrepreneur Lifestyle with great Health, Wealth & Relations.

Idea is useless, execution is everything.

Self- investment is the best investment you can ever make.

You can have anything, it's a matter of how bad you want.

Start Early, Sometimes you got to run before you can walk.

This World starts with you, Ends with you, It's All Yours.....

www.ingramcontent.com/pod-product-compliance
Lightning Source LLC
Chambersburg PA
CBHW020607220526
45463CB00006B/2487